Shoe Music Press

 Published and printed in the USA by Shoe Music Press, P.O. Box 4641 Alpharetta, GA 30023.

Visit us online at www.shoemusicpress.com

Cover Image by Toni Frissel, taken at Weeki Wachee Springs, FL 1947 (in the public domain and courtesy of Wikimedia Commons).

Title page image "Tree of Knowledge" by Johnny Automatic, courtesy of www.openclipart.org

Table of Contents with notes by the author

poem never resolves into the conflagration it is building towards. Instead, it leaves the reader with a sense of unresolved frustration but also of future possibilities, exactly the way an initial meeting with someone you are wildly attracted to often ends in a delay of passion.

Dalliance is about the emotional/spiritual relationship between the lovers and the intimate flirtations that lead to consummation, rather than the act itself. The poem is written from the POV of a Princess encouraging a long-awaited tryst with her princely lover. Affairs of state have kept them from private moments for too long. She entreats him to forgo the duties of the royal court for a while and find renewed passion in her arms. And so the dalliance begins.

Although the poem is about a royal couple and begins with subtler allusions to sex (such as "surrendering my maiden's favor" and "partake of my gifts"), the inherent meaning can be applied to most couples (after all every man is said to be king of his castle and most young women like to think of themselves as princesses sometimes. Thus enters the fantasy/romance element). "Dalliance" serves as a reminder to lovers not to let work or other obligations overwhelm one so much that truly important matters, such as love, go unattended for too long.

Nocturne Rhapsody tells of a voyage into the world of night where two nocturnal creatures—a nymph and a vampire—meet in the shadows. Both women flirt and tempt each other until the literal physical journey of the nymph, who is new to this place of darkness, shifts toward another kind of physical expedition, one that leads into the realm of the sensual. Their night together leads to the nymph's discovery that she has also been on an emotional journey the whole time. She has found a friend rather than merely a lover for an evening. Though their parting is filled with sadness, the knowledge of this connection leaves room for hope that they will meet again.

Together is about discovering a bond with another lost soul. The speaker of the poem sees beyond the surface of her lover and by taking a closer look recognizes similarities between herself and a chance met partner in lust. This lust transforms into so much more once she has glimpsed a reflection of herself in someone else. Both lovers have been made poignantly beautiful by previous sorrow and look to each other as a bastion against loneliness. The speaker, driven by the possibility that someone can understand her past pain, coaxes the object of her desire to reveal more of herself because she trusts that "the desperate search for peace ends in each other's arms."

Reunion 21

Reunion shows a glimpse of two lovers in bed after an incident in which they had broken up for a time. The woman is rhapsodizing about their re-found love, as she snuggles close to her lover. She feels blest to be back in his arms. In the last line, she speaks of "claiming that last kiss you never gave me," which refers back to when they had first broken up and he had refused to kiss her farewell. Now, she has claimed that kiss and in doing so, brought them back into reunion.

Love's Expression 22

Love's Expression is about sensuality and love blended in good measure. The poem follows a recipe, not unlike a satisfying four course meal. The feast of sensations leads from basking in each other's presence, to flirtation, through the act of making love, to the dénouement into cuddling. At the end, the speaker of the poem praises her lover because he is always so communicative of his love and she offers this poem as "a taste of my love's expression."

Once More.. 24

Once More focuses on a woman who, despite the fact that she and her lover have broken up, cannot help returning to him to fall back into bed. She knows that the encounter is purely sexual because her lover cared "just enough to let me go" because he couldn't remain faithful. Still she feels the warmth of his lips, tastes his tongue, smells the scent of his skin, and so falls hopelessly back into his arms against her own good judgment. This poem speaks of the addictive nature of love/lust. The woman knows that their relationship is over; still she recognizes the aroma of "Once My Lover" and cannot help but give herself to him again even if just for one night.

Banquet for Two 27

Banquet for Two is quite literally a decadent feast. The poem begins with a kiss and continues with allusions to food and eating throughout. A large part of the poem is dedicated to the mouth and its inherent part in sexual play. Whether the references are to licking or to nibbling, to a lover's "palate" or to the "spiced flavor" of his skin, the poem is rife with allusions to taste. There are five courses, each of which corresponds to stanza, served in this banquet of "consuming" passion. From the appetizer of kissing through the meatier portions to the rich dessert of the afterglow, this poem is meant to show delight in the carnal feast.

Moonlight Rendezvous.. 31

Moonlight Rendezvous can be viewed as a symphony of sensations. The two lovers are the instruments, together making sweet music. The poem has four movements, each with its own tempo to set the pace. The tempo affects not only the speed but also the mood and the difficulty of a symphonic piece (or of a sexual rendezvous). The first movement is soft and slow, the second playful, the third intense in tone, and the fourth brings the music and the lovers to a satisfying climax.

Please let me see the depths of who you are.

Midnight Pleasures

ACT I

Kiss by kiss, I journey across your burning form.
Pacing, my mouth craves the taste of your flesh.
My sleek figure prowling over your responsive body.
Silently, in the passing shadows our silhouettes enmesh.

Hunting for your hot mouth in the dark night,
the delights of which are like the moon in full.
Star-strewn ecstasies adorn the sky with white fire,
when I feel the energetic surge of your lips' pull.

Your kisses, nibbled like clusters of savory fruits,
bruise against my lips, smearing juices succulent.
Your caresses like wind in the wheat brush over me.
Sumptuous aroma of a full, heady wine is your scent.

Your arms enclose me, drawing me to your firm chest.
Together, wrapped in love, the moments are lavish.
You turn us over as the Autumn wind chases the leaf,
so that you are above, a better pose in which to ravish.

I am gently crushed beneath you on the soft sheets.
Your hips, pressed close to mine in a kiss of fire.
Firm thigh sliding beneath the light touch of my hand.
Our souls and bodies locked into the rhythms of desire.

Pulsing like the tide that washes with ebbs and flows.
Drumming against the shoreline of my pale body,
which palpitates with hurried breaths, escaping sighs,
as the waves from a flood of pleasure rush in to fill me.

(Continued on page 2)

2

The clash of lightning takes us both with a shock,
electrifying heightened sensations, flashing swift.
The pulsing in the veins subsides slowly, like a storm.
We lie tangled, recovering from the intense divine gift.

My fingers trace along your back, run through your hair,
lazily skimming your form, as we lie in blissful opulence.
Enjoying the cooling of our flushed skin and spirits,
as we lie embracing, my thoughts return to decadence.

The embers of my lust spark again as though fanned.
My desire for you is like a crimson rose in bloom.
My longing, like lambent flames, burns in the hearth,
blazing, retreating, waiting eagerly to consume.

ACT II

You stand before me, as naked as a husked chestnut,
and I worship at your altar with offerings of pleasure.
Loving you in this secret place between the shadows,
where the spicy incense of your skin is mine to treasure.

My mouth sweetly caresses your throbbing flesh,
sustaining, not yet sating, my appetite for you.
Hungrily, I devour the honey of your essence,
and savor the moisture of your body's bejeweled dew.

The music of your sighs paired with soft moans thrills me.
You are empowered by my surrender, yet you tremble still,
as though rapt, or wracked, or else on that liminal brink,
almost over-pouring against your own half-sensible will.

My tongue bewitches with its talents, expertly timed—
tracing your terrain, lavishly licking, drawing you in,
pulling away, teasing, only to push you deeper inside,
until my purpose is gained and your goal won again.

Spilling your opalescence, like cream into a waiting cup.
    The vessel of my mouth, as though starving, drinks deep.
Love, spread the flavor of your sincere ardor through me,
    for, your satiated pleasure is the reward that I reap.

Just as I honor the charms of each enchanted evening,
    let us relish and bask in the taste of one another's delight.
Silver intentions melt to golden rest as dozing moonbeams,
    hold in sway fleeting magic for just the hour of midnight.

Shadow Lover

I have a secret that I keep.
My silence all these years
has been a burden and a blessing.
But the oath is worth the tears.

I have a shadow lover,
who steals to me by night.
I hold him in my arms till dawn.
He vanishes with the light.

I know but the name he whispers.
I know not the sight of his face.
But together in the darkness,
my chamber is a lovely place.

I discern by touching his countenance
that his face is youthful and fine.
His visage is smooth and flawless.
And this soothes doubts of mine.

But his skin is all shadow,
yet lit with pale white fire.
Muscles hard and sleek glow,
inflaming my desire.

Strong and lithe is his body.
And wings hover o'er his back.
I shiver at this shadowy canopy,
which in the night looms deeper black.

His hair cascades around me.
I am veiled by the darkened cloak.
His wings whisper in windless dark.
His embrace is the ghost touch of smoke.

Yet I fall to his caresses,
as though I am under a heavy spell.
Drowsily I begin to wonder
if my lover is a fallen angel.

Or perhaps he's some celestial,
such as Eros fair and free.
Come in soft and shadowy form
to make another Psyche of me.

I know not if I consort with demons.
I wantonly do not care.
He makes love to me like a god
and lifts me into the air.

He bites my flesh so sweetly,
and plays my body like a flute.
He drinks my kisses like ambrosia,
until my moans become mute.

But he slips away with the morning.
And I awaken in my tangled bed alone.
My shadow lover dissolves with dawn.
His true self still, as yet, unknown.

We've met in tryst each night for years.
He says he cannot come to me by day.
"Your world is not for me," he declares,
"The daylight will always banish me away."

Thus I must take him at his word
and hold him while I can when he is near.
For he may be some dream I've spun,
because once at dawn I saw him disappear.

A burden and a privilege it is
to be the secret lover of the divine.
Be he demon, angel, or dream,
I thank the universe that he is mine.

6

The Very First Time

Like a flower on the threshold of blooming,
Yet still threatened by a late frost,
I stood on the brink of womanhood,
Shrouded in darkness, caught between two voids,
I vacillated, filled with doubt and confusion,

Then, I felt your hand take hold of mine,
Pulling me safely into the sanctuary of your arms,
My heart fluttered like a frightened dove,
Still, you held me close against your chest,
The rhythm of your steady heartbeat,
Like an opiate, calming my restlessness,

I allowed myself to sink into your embrace,
Long dark hair, yet lighter than the shadows,
Which had threatened to consume me,
Was a fragrant veil, filled with the scents,
Of pines and wheat—the odors of roaming,

Windswept straying locks, shielded my face,
As I burrowed into your neck for protection,
Storms raged and then passed on, leaving us,
To search for fulfillment in each other,
Both having been exiled into bitter isolation,

We understood one another's suffering,
Both alone, now together, solaced by compassion,
Which allowed us to bond implicitly, without words,
For the very first time, I felt truly seen and accepted,
By a man who cared for me, and the world seemed gentler,

We wove a friendship from star-gazing and memories,
Nature walks and storytelling, talking late into the night,
Weathering tempests, and quiet times spent cuddling,
Your hand stroked my hair, as we spoke of dreams,

And when the future arose as the subject of discussion,
I looked eagerly to you, for the support of a friend,
Yet I saw in your dark eyes a glint of something more,

Deep within those pools, an intention, like sunken treasure,
Prospect as yet unexplored, still I knew that it was of gold,
So, transfixed by possibility, I continued to dive,
Into the watery realm, eager to discover this new wealth,
Yet I blushed to think upon it, and we both turned away,

But time and again I noticed that *I* gave that same rich look,
And every so often I detained your unsuspecting glance,
Then you smiled so tenderly—half secret, half revealing,
And led your eyes down and away, yet still smiling,

Until finally neither of us could doubt nor deny,
So during a gaze we were drawn inevitably together,
Your mouth met mine in warm, undulating delight,
Your strong arms gathered me up, clasping me to you,
For the very first time, I felt truly beautiful and supported,
And the warmth of your body ran through me like a river,
Making the world a sweet and lovely place to reside,

We grew ever closer as friends, but the enticement lingered,
Over months that swept by like water over a cascade,
And you waited for our feelings to slowly bud and ripen,
Content that the never fading spark flared sometimes,
Like a meteor that remains visible in the sky for days,

We each made a secret wish upon that shooting star,
And gentle hands, cupping one another, grew bolder,
Until I placed myself in your trust, as you laid me down,
Your fingers, like a blind man, caressing the petals of a lily,
Feeling carefully for the sensations of my reactions,

(Continued on page 8)

8

Slowly, tenderly, and with many a fond look,
Which weighed my responses of surrender to pleasure,
With the slightest trembling of my virgin body,
You peeled away my clothing, with the mildest touch,
Eyes and words calm, patiently asking permission,
In tones as rich as dark chocolate melting off your tongue,

And I let my hands pass over your naked flesh—
Chest and arms smooth, your candlelit copper skin aglow,
Your body seeming powerful in its natural state,
A contrast to mine, which like porcelain, seemed fragile,
Yet, I knew that this was your first time as well,
Although I could not read the mysteries of your heart,

You soothed me with gentle, unhurried hands,
Reassuring me with that velvet voice, deep like the ocean,
Stilling my soul until it was fully prepared to mingle,
Along with our bodies in a sensuous embrace,

You whispered in my ear and I nodded my consent,
Then you pulled me to you, our hearts coupled in a dance,
Touching, kissing, tasting, making love—
For the very first time, I felt desired and loved,
And the world with all its wonders fell away.

Trance

Fixated by those entrancing eyes,
magnetic blue, they hypnotize.

Let all the world around them haze,
I am lost in their penetrating gaze.

A nervous dove, I am suddenly disarmed,
enrapt and frozen—by the cobra charmed.

My body tense, as thoughts fly askew,
lost in the swirl of an intense azure hue.

I feel your force like twin moons in full,
drowning me in a relentless whirlpool.

Sable locks frame a seductive countenance.
I am electrified by the invisible currents,

sparking between our eyes when they meet,
an encounter so bold as to be indiscreet.

An instant wave of powerful attraction,
acts with a spiraling centrifugal reaction,

strewing out possibilities for a moment,
if only we both dissolved into consent.

Undeniable temptation like lambent flames,
we greet each other, exchanging names.

Here, I am Rapture and you are Trance,
limitless pleasures caught in a glance.

(Continued on page 10)

10

The symmetry of our epithets you notice,
compared together, we are states of bliss.

This coincidence prompts me to be forthright,
"Well I am certainly entranced tonight,

and if our fortunes be twined with allure,
perhaps later on you'll be *in* Rapture."

One brow raised, impressed by my allusion,
the chemistry between us luring us to fusion.

Lingering on thoughts of the unexplored,
your knowing smile is the best reward.

You laud me orally on my quick wit,
confirming delicious options infinite.

The laurels of your mouth are but one desire,
that deep within me your face and form inspire.

All in due time, yet the ecstasies that await,
consume me, inflaming my heightened state.

We part for a time, yet as I muse on chance,
my eyes are drawn back to your easy stance.

Beguiling in its poise, yet casual, and idiosyncratic,
your smooth gestures and charms so charismatic—

a gothic angel, refined incubus, or twilit muse,
who arouses thoughts of future rendezvous.

Dark as midnight and as pale as the moon,
insinuating mysteries like an ancient rune.

I watch you on stage, your presence has emphasis,
as you perform many a rehearsed metamorphosis.

From mad scientist to slave to coin-operated boy,
each time adding a new fantasy for me to enjoy.

The white lab-coat, then dark shades, later black leather,
the Violet Wand instruments made for pleasure,

kept in your pocket like devices purely scientific,
tempt me with expectations like visions beatific.

Kindling lust internally harbored and hidden,
inciting thoughts that are surely forbidden.

Lust swells, flooding me, at the idea of the taboo,
an illicit song starts and I come for you.

The touch of your hand enhances my arousal.
We move together decadently like at a bacchanal.

My body sways with this new found Trance.
Music crashes and lights flash as we dance,

flooding the room with light and sound.
But under your influence I am bound,

Industrial, metal, techno—the sensual Fetish feast.
On the dance floor our souls are finally released,

from mortal fetters to meet in a tryst.
Incarnate, my lips yearn to be kissed,

overwhelming me with unbearable passion.
I reach out to find our mouths in union.

Tongues mingling along with savory essence.
We burn in a conflagration of concupiscence.

(Continued on page 12)

12

Needing to douse the raging inferno,
we are doomed to ash unless we let go.

Too many more pleasures yet to be had,
so we end for now, awaiting the myriad.

Transient Trance, transcendental evermore,
must leave before we can truly explore.

Always liminal, I fear I have lost my chance,
for by definition an enrapturing Trance,

is an ideal that lies somewhere in between,
a vision and a memory, an illusion and a dream.

Dalliance

Your face, soft with love, beckons me to you like a flame.
Alluring eyes charm and sway me with their flirtatious glance.
A charismatic smile allays my honor's wavering defenses.
You give me *that look*, against which I've never stood a chance.

Your keen eyes can pierce the veils of modesty,
that I've hung around my heart to hide my true intent.
Seeing past my demure manners with your intuition,
which knows that coy flirtations will dissolve into consent.

Softly yielding to your attentions—such enticing courtesies.
Surrendering my maiden's favor, effortlessly won.
Instinctively you sense my secret yearning for us to bond.
Understanding my needs with your natural wisdom.

Just for now: disregard propriety, release your inhibitions,
dismiss your guards and send away your courtly retinue,
throw off your mantle of decorum, brush aside obligation.
Leave the world behind; I just want to be alone with you.

Free yourself from time's chains; enter instead our sacred realm.
Society can live without you for a time, however I cannot.
Welcome to our private temple, the domain of love's intimacy.
Here we can revel in sensual delight, pleasure as our only thought.

Still, chivalry obliges you to press your lips first to my hand.
Paying homage with a kiss—a noble gesture that is courtesy's due.
To consecrate this moment, you offer tribute by bestowing a token.
I receive the silver keepsake, accepting the dance of our rendezvous.

(Continued on page 14)

14

Your hair—golden stardust—cascades around my face, soothing me.
Still, I blush at the touch of your warm lips as you bend to claim your accolade.
Coaxing my mouth open to enjoyment with your gentle influences,
before your tongue, with its own enchantments, begins to serenade.

Allow this longing to tease and indulge, lost in abandon.
While our bodies, supple with desire, hunger to unite.
As your Lady-fair I invite you to partake of my gifts—
a cherished reward to you, My Prince, and worthiest knight.

Intermingling our essences, submerged in a lusty ocean.
Fusing our passions with kisses of fire, ever mounting in pace.
Filling the ache of separate skins with spiritual communion.
Eagerly our limbs entangle in the most intimate embrace.

Lying naked together in our clandestine, hallowed sphere.
Our souls bond, as our bodies merge, in a closeness I have missed.
My thoughts are only of us; the outside world has vanished.
Time has stilled for our hidden hearts while we dally in our tryst.

Nocturne Rhapsody

In the darkness after midnight,
you appeared to me through the mist,
and danced against my swaying figure,
tempting me until we finally kissed.

Creamy caramel skin sweet to the taste,
covering the sensuous slip of a body,
with gentle curves like lowland hills.
Your liquid brown eyes seduced me.

The blush of roses formed a succulent mouth,
that bit hungrily with the fangs of a vampire.
My neck sucked hard for blood or passion.
Your gothic eyes were aflame with desire.

And my lust grew apace with the moments,
so that when you had to leave from there,
I followed you, My Night-flown Goddess,
and invited you back to a private lair.

Once in my chambers we quickly unleashed,
our slender forms from black leather clothes.
You stood like a knight's divine vision,
with the easy beauty that only a Kindred knows.

Dusky hair shining like polished obsidian,
a lock the hue of moon-shadow fell in your face,
seductively veiling one entrancing eye,
which whispered of never leaving this place.

So we sank into the depths of each other,
sensual touching of soft bodies pressed,
together enmeshed in an tumult of pleasure,
I saw the holy Trinity and felt myself blessed.

(Continued on page 16)

16

Naked in the light, I beheld your wings,
wondering if you were succubus or angel.
In awe, I let your fingers drift over me,
and satisfy my lust as it began to swell.

I took your willowy form into my arms,
and found the bloodlines of a Dark Princess,
which cause her to need the freedom of being alone.
Yet she can be strong enough to open to gentleness.

So on your smooth cheek I placed a kiss,
and reverently worshiped each breast.
Nibbling pert nipples and moving down.
I let my mouth serenade the rest.

My lips glided over your tempting flesh,
until I found the source I searched for.
I buried my face in your open essence,
listening eagerly to your moans begging for more.

Gasping pants and a musical chirping,
accompanied by occasional finishing sighs.
Back arched, you drowned in your rapture.
Eyelashes flurried like sable butterflies.

Blood flushed lips quivered like a young dove,
who is preparing for her first unsteady flight.
Emotions swirled in vivid colors of warmth,
as our bodies joined together in the night.

Amidst your shuddering ecstasies time was lost.
Hours passed immersed in bliss without rest.
Slim legs and arms entwined in a dance,
as I kissed long neck, flat belly, orbed breast.

And your mouth found my responsive places,
with lips sucking or the lapping of your tongue.
So my body trembled and my spirit rose,
to where pan pipes play and nymphs revels are sung.

17

Then you laid your head down on my lap,
with a serenity like a half becoming whole,
and our bodies like twin shadows revolved,
each around the beauty of the other's soul.

Our fingers danced upon one another's skin,
as our mouths met for a wine-sweet kiss.
My hands traced the supple body of the girl,
whom I knew I would soon achingly miss.

Passion sated for a while, we mingled fingers.
Cuddling closely, we lay a long while in bed,
our faces and lips alternately pressed together.
I melted each time you kissed my forehead.

Lingering, we talked, sharing pieces of soul,
and I saw that our spirits were the same—
we both longed for the comfort of caring.
So to me you revealed your true name.

I trembled like a fawn at its rare beauty,
and for joy that you handed me such trust,
so I will hold your unmasked self sacred,
as a sincere friend or lover always must.

By morning, we both had to fly away,
as night's children at daybreak must do,
but we gave to each other a beacon,
so you might find me and I might find you.

Paradise was contained in that night,
and we were both hesitant to let it end,
kissing fervently, fingers still grasping,
ecstatically ready to start our evening again.

Though our journeys have taken us apart,
we may still meet some night under the moon.
Missing you, I have launched my signal flare,
and you have said that you will come soon.

18

Together

In the night tide that engulfs us, your eyes glitter like black diamonds,
the stars are jealous of the infinity they hold.
Your smile, half-knowing, intrigues my heart.
The flush of a scarlet promise invites me to trace your lips,
as yielding as the petals of a flourishing rose.
The taste of your mouth like cherries in all their delicious charm.
The poetry of your skin unfolds like calligraphy beneath the brush of my fingertips.
I cup my hands over orbed breasts, which play the Music of Spheres as I caress them.
The flat of your belly like the golden plains of the West—of which I've only dreamed.
Your curves as gentle as the cooing of doves.
My thirst for you burns unquenchable.
The bonfire of my soul responds to the flames in your eyes.

Yet, your memory is made of smoke and shadow, tingling at the edge of sensation.
I remember how you touched the loneliness of my soul,
the deserted beach of a solitary isle, which I know you have seen yourself.
Your tender curves made me forget my sorrow.
In your arms, I felt like a child come home.
I saw through the mask of your name,
and the camouflage of your garments fell away.
Then I glimpsed the burning luminescence of a radiant soul.
But your spirit constantly flies away with the night, journeying far off,
leaving your sensuous body to find comfort on its own.
You are inhabited by echoes when your eyes turn distant,
but my spirit soars too when night rides his black stallion.

We meet in flight like two nightingales, tumbling back to our bodies.
In your mysterious eyes, I behold the Land of Dreams.
My spirit dances with you under a full moon,
on the sand of a beach that we can both share.
Your ebony hair—smooth as satin—slips through my fingers as I reach for a kiss.
Your skin, like caramel, begs to be tasted.
And you open like a flower in bloom to my gentle touch,
as I drink the sweet ambrosia of your essence.
You fit my fingers like a handmade Italian leather glove,

yet more precious is the flesh that envelops my hand.

You give yourself over to rapture again and again,
eyelashes fluttering like waves of midnight-tinted butterflies.
Your moans, coaxed like the notes from a Stradivarius,
are in perfect pitch as though a violin could know the ecstasy of the musician,
at performing the strokes that create the sweetest tones.
Pleasing you, I am enthralled; like being immersed in the "Moonlight Sonata,"
a masterpiece played with nimble fingers,
which winds me in a spell so potent that my mind is rapt, my body motionless,
my spirit dancing enchanted, as my soul takes wing.
I can do nothing but listen to such a masterpiece,
and fall in love with the melody time and time again.

After hours of strumming the music of one another's pleasure,
we knew the moon had set on our time together.
The solitude of our seas came rushing in like the inevitable tide.
We were still drunk with the passion we shared, tangled in shadows and dreams,
and we both saw each other clearly through the masquerade of the ball.
I beheld a lonely girl as though looking in a mirror,
I saw myself reflected in your eyes of absence.
Silence full of sadness like when a moonflower perishes.

I lament that you are willow at the Lake of Weeping Dreamers,
with tears turned to leaves falling into a still pool.
Yet the waters of your soul listen for the sound of the waves' spray.
I too have shed tears in that pool, longing for another to see me.
But as a Knight of Infinite Resignation I cannot be my own savior,
I wander lost amidst a forest of statues—Stones-of-no-Resolve.
One of them appears to be hardening into your visage,
and I beat my sword against my breast to no avail.

Perhaps the flickering flames of our spirits, which drown in our own melted wax,
can be poured into the cupped hands of each other.
Together we can free ourselves to burn as bright as our busheled souls released.
Unwrap the absence in which you drape yourself.
Step from the shadows of your solitude.

(Continued on page 20)

20

I will meet you there standing with my naked soul,
because I believe we can heal each other's wounds.

You are a rose in a barren landscape, and I am a wanderer here.
I bring water so that we may both drink deeply.
Your rare beauty will nourish my spirit beyond a draught from the purest fountain.
Let our souls be thirsty for someone else.
Together we can fill the emptiness with moonlight and strands of pearls,
with room to dance, moving as one, while the piano plays itself,
together in a glass room looking out to the sea.

Or else we can step out onto the terrace and let the zephyrs,
with soft, trembling kisses or deep swallowing passion,
tangle our hair together, in flowing tresses of mingled eclipse and sunlight.
We can splash in the foam that shimmers along the beach.
The waves of your soul roll out to lure me.
Please let me see the depths of who you are.

I am as vulnerable as a moth in the light of your presence,
I fear my wings will be torn by your rejection.
I will not abandon you if you will do the same for me.
Open the bud of your exotic lily and allow me to see the true you.
I promise to be gentle with the petals of your soul,
for the longings that your heart holds mirror mine.
I believe that the desperate search for peace ends in each other's arms,
and the veil will drop from our glazed eyes so we can see life's beauty once more.
Together, let us turn the darkness in on itself until it flees.
Together, let us release laughter back into our world.
Together we will have the strength because we will not be alone.

Reunion

Once more, in holy kiss we are wed,
Whispers of heaven touch us again,
Back between satin sheets on your bed,
Angel's caress—the silky touch of skin on skin,
The warmth of our bodies pressed together,
Forms an aura around us—a soft halo,
Fingers intertwined, or tips traced like a feather,
We bask in Love's reforged, hazy glow,
Memories of these sensations wash over me,
Renewed as I once again feel the rapture,
Undulating waves on a rediscovered sea,
Sated, yet hungrier, as each feeling I recapture,
A sacred hush falls as we embrace,
I savor your warm breath upon my flesh,
And study the tranquility of your face,
Our bodies, ever thirsting for each other, enmesh,
Longing looks, heavy with the ambrosia of love,
Show desire rekindled and yet also sated,
Misted eyes, now clearer, glint with light from above,
Finding once more the long awaited,
Drinking deeply of each other's sighs,
Running fingers through soft strands of hair,
Our hearts and bodies have become wise,
Tenderly touching skin and souls that are bare,
Naked, enrapt we lay for a while,
As our heartbeats slow to a steady pace,
We both share a lazy, contented smile,
As we hold each other in this timeless place,
Waiting quietly for sweet slumber, we rest,
Soon to be ferried across Morpheus's stream,
We have reunited in a love twice blessed,
So sweet and longed for it feels like a dream,
May I never awaken from this sleep of bliss if that be so,
Let me linger in this Paradise for eternity,
Rediscovering the communion we lost long ago,
Renewed by me claiming that last kiss you never gave me.

Love's Expression

When I look into your blue-green eyes,
which are brimming with love for me,
time is stilled and I lose myself
on the gentle waves of their aqua sea.

Clear and bright, defenses unraveled,
a soft innocence within unfolds to create
a resonating, hazy glow of adoration
and a spark of desire that cannot wait.

Unmasked, we see each other's souls
and smile to see tentativeness released.
Our spirits reach out to touch each other
as our bodies' desire for contact is increased.

My heart trembles to see your smiling dimples.
Shivers ensue when you flash that nodding grin,
which is full of "come hither" confidence
and signals our dance of flirtation to begin.

Soft lips caress one another and I quiver.
Your hand tenderly cradles my face,
then traces the contours of my body
before you pull me into a tight embrace.

You spell out delights with your tongue,
breathing gentle words against my flesh.
With a tremor, your essence flows into me,
while tangled in a lover's knot, we enmesh.

You whisper of how much you love me
and I return your words with adoring sighs.
As I gaze dreamily, your face is like a vision
and I drown in the pools that are your eyes.

I return from their depths, still captivated.
Both of your cheeks, now softly kissed.
Inhaling the arousing scent of your skin,
which makes me giddy, so I can't resist
another passionate meeting of mouths.

Never sated but always satisfied.
Snuggling, I savor the peacefulness
that your warm, safe arms provide.

This moment is precious, so I linger,
quietly listening to your steady heartbeat.
Riding the rise and fall of your breath,
that lulls me into a slumber honeysweet.

In my dreams, I remember your charming voice,
singing classic melodies of romantic affection.
You always seem to say the words I need to hear,
so now, here is a taste of my love's expression.

Once More

1

The soft pressure of your mouth upon mine,
The warmth of your soft lip's skin,
The sweet taste of your exhaled breath,
Your gentle tongue, and here I am again,
Enfolded in your arms' tender embrace,
My senses overwhelmed and overjoyed,
I feel myself dropping into the flood,
Of feelings I swore I would avoid,
Just one kiss and the world dissolves,
Leaving us alone among stars in the night,
I thought we could just touch lips to lips,
And reason still triumph over this delight.

2

We melt like wax into each other, mixing,
Hot, free-flowing, smooth, and decadent,
I nibble your lip, your neck, your ear,
Your flesh is dewy and divinely succulent,
I recognize your aroma as "Once My Lover,"
And the deluge of passion washes over me,
I had resigned myself never to hold you again,
But now your touch lingers on my face longingly,
I see the ache in your eyes, knowing it is also in mine,
As you run your fingers through my lush hair,
I slip out of my clothes and peel off yours,
So we are holding each other, our bodies bare.

3

Though you are no longer mine to hold,
Every time I see your dearly loved face,
All my inhibitions are stripped away,
And I fall once more into your embrace,
I thought I could stay distant from you,
Away from all the charms that I adore,

I tired to annul my golden memories,
Yet here I am like so many times before.

4

As we fall on the bed, I feel my soul naked,
My heart's armor undone by your tender caress,
Though my mind knows this is just for one night,
Your belovéd voice whispers and I must acquiesce,
I believed I had put aside doting emotions,
Dull to the pain that had been my downfall,
You loved me once, just enough to let me go,
Because you didn't care enough to stay loyal,
The heat of your body against mine, doubled,
Raises the foolish idea that this is where I belong,
The feeling of us pressed together in wanton lust,
Pricks the pain of knowing my love is still strong.

5

My mouth moves over your exposed flesh,
Slowly over fondly remembered places,
Lapping, I breathe in your private scent,
Over sensitive spots my tongue playfully traces,
Indulging you more, I feel you tremble,
I know this means you are on the brink,
Holding back your explosion of rapture,
I catch your eye, staring deeply, and wink,
Feeling the outpour of your pent-up elation,
I savor the taste of your divine essence,
Then take you, still shivering, into my arms,
Because your release was so intense.

6

Though you are no longer mine to hold,
Every time I see your dearly loved face,
All my inhibitions are stripped away,
And I fall once more into your embrace,

(Continued on page 26)

I thought I could stay distant from you,
Away from all the charms that I adore,
I tried to annul my golden memories,
Yet here I am like so many times before.

7

Fingers entwine as we begin a slow rhythm,
I listen with satisfaction to your sighs,
We lay joined in the most natural fashion,
I take hold just to watch your look of surprise,
That dreamy glaze and gentle parting of the lips,
Then the way your eyes glint looking down at me,
Impressed and elated, riding the crest of a high,
On the waves of a tide of carnal ecstasy,
You roll me softly among the covers,
The signal to enter into the forbidden,
Pressing gently, you push your way inside,
And I surrender to the strong pulsing within.

8

The afterglow—we lay in the damp warmth,
Your arms cuddling me, wrapping me in bliss,
My head on your chest, the waves of your breath,
I lay thinking "How can I live without this?"
Then my heart is pierced to the core knowing,
That this moment of comfort will end soon,
All the riches of the world plus a hundred lovers,
Could not heal nor even staunch this deep wound,
I grow numb and stumbling, my tears begin to fall,
Knowing this is but a covert visit with my paramour,
You no longer want to be part of a family together,
I will go home, but first give me the illusion once more.

Banquet for Two

You seal our lover's pact with kisses
of sweet fire, upon the vellum of my body.
Outlining my curves and contours.
Mapping the terrain—hills, valleys, and delta
—with teasing licks that cross the wild-lands
which span the region of my private domain.
First, moistening this hidden province with bold licks,
that unfold the petals of my exotic flower.
Nudging them to spread open so as to receive
the balmy sunrays of your attention.
You teasingly swirl around, fluent in tongue-play,
then nip and pull lovingly until I reach the crest
of an amorous wave, riding atop until its collapse.
Next, you taunt me by dipping into my hot-spring,
doling out the smooth tasting honeyed-syrup
only to be found in this concealed source.
The glazed liqueur drizzles onto your palate
as you indulge in delectably wanton banquet.
Still, I have more personal sweets to relish
and dessert has yet to be served.

So, my sultry mouth returns favor for favor—
tongue dallying over your responsive flesh,
fondly lapping and flickering like a soft flame.
Gently teasing your taut hardness.
I find the spiced flavor of your skin irresistible.
As I tickle and trace, I am enticed to sample
the dewdrop nectar of your essence,
Inspired by sizzling temptation to new pursuits,
I allow my lips to part and slowly take in
the pinnacle of your erotic column.
I slide along the stately pillar to its base,
drawing you in and pulling away again.

(Continued on page 28)

28

Wreathing that superior lance of adamant
with the garland of my mouth
in honor of the gallant champion of my heart.
I enjoy sucking on your enhanced arousal,
first with shallow caresses,
cresting the ridge with my zealous tongue,
then diving under the ledge to lick furiously
but with precision over your most sensitive spot
until you almost release that pent-up energy
that must remain unexpressed for a time.
With unrelenting vigor, I begin bobbing my head,
doting upon your pulsing flesh and its divine flavor.
My insistency is intoxicating, as I sheath
your sovereign broadsword to the hilt.
Letting you revel in the deeper delights of my mouth.
I have a weakness for pleasuring you.
So my body electrifies at the sensation of you
convulsing within my throat during climax.
I become so hot from feeling your indulgence,
that with a dexterous hand on my center of desire,
fondling and rubbing, I bring myself to conclusion.
The rumbling sound of my appreciation is vocalized
as I swallow all the delicious creaminess you outpour
to the sounds of your uninhibited moaning.

After a short interlude, I am impressed to see
that you are hardly finished and stand ready once again.
I look admiringly upon the heroic prize—
a paragon of majesty with which nobility
has so generously endowed you.
My impulse is to touch and stroke with affection
that rigid firmness by which I know you intimately.
Urged on by low murmurs and hushed sighs,
My hand ascends and descends your stately tower—
a tribute you deserve for your romantic chivalry.
As I caress you, your hands affectionately traverse
the curves of my abundant cleavage.

My instinctual excitement is piqued
by you tugging lightly on the dainty buds
that crown the summits of those silken rises.
Skimming the crescent hollow of my hip,
while my thoughts flirt with intriguing possibilities.
You press yourself firmly against my yielding body.
I can feel your smoldering need become feverish.
As the flames of ardor envelop us, I know that
my enthusiasm is roused for more tantalizing fare.

Our passion flares, consuming
the familiar world around us
in a scarlet blaze of concupiscence.
Nothing remains except our awareness
of two bodies locked together in a fervent ritual
of longing and fulfillment,
thirst and quenching, ache and satisfaction.
You take command of my body
with the certainty of a king.
My flesh is the center of your domain—
the lavish palace you inhabit
wherein you brandish the scepter of regal authority.
Wielding the lusty power of your arousal
with consummate expertise.
I defer to your virile energy
as each thrust delves deeper into my wet promise.
Soon, our lively frolicking picks up momentum,
becoming boisterous romping for a time.
Finally, our gamboling transforms
into a frenzied culmination of intense reactions.
Delight thrills through me like a shaft of lightning,
igniting my heightened senses until they erupt
in a midnight conflagration.
You gush into me and we lie entangled, gasping.

(Continued on page 30)

30

My soul dances like a butterfly on a zephyr—
weightless and free, winging adoringly
around our bodies—enmeshed in a lover's knot.
Your eyes have flown away
into the white hum of bliss,
leaving your body trembling in my arms
while you are rapt and wandering in abandon.
I reach to kiss your forehead as you breathe softly.
My love for you overflows its banks yet again,
as I watch your serene face, drifting in peace.
I ache to join you, as your tranquility infuses me.
The stars illuminate our bower as we sleep
and our dreams, saturated with love, intermingle.

Moonlight Rendezvous

1.

An eloquent glance reveals that
I catch the fancy of your nocturnal regard.
Fixed within those burning eyes,
I see the intensity of your longing
and shiver at the magnetic force
of the allure that you wield instinctively.
Beguiling me with spell-like charms.

Such charismatic influence naturally
wins me with gentle persuasion.
Blushing, I await your advances.
My heart whispers of pleasures soon to come.

Your touch—respectful but eager—
traces my cheeks, my lips, my throat.
Gaze lingering on my face,
as your eyes kindle with desire.

Shaking off that customary reserve,
you pull me, irresistibly, into your arms.
Flirtatiously nibbling my neck.
I sigh and shiver, my hunger sparked,
while you devour my sumptuous mouth.

During our steamy embrace,
I succumb to your amorous intent.
Immersed in sensual caresses.
I find myself laid bare beneath your lithe form—
positioned over me with the prowess of a warrior.
My supine figure outstretched,
back arched and breathless,
as your fingers brush across my exposed flesh.

(Continued on page 32)

Slender arms entwine with strong ones,
our fingers interlaced, palms pressed together,
as our bodies seek the warm welcome of each other,
Wandering hands ascend shapely mounds—
ample and round—cupping them appreciatively
as deeper sensations awaken in a tingling rush.

2.

I surrender my body into your keeping.
Your mouth pursues a downward course,
lapping and nibbling my tender skin
until you arrive at my quivering thighs.
Teasing around the source of your desire,
for moments that linger with anticipation
before your face nestles into my succulence.

Your tongue, orchestral and divine,
sparks my passion to the ravenous appetite
of a wildfire consuming the forest.
You take pleasure in my arousing responses—
sighs escaping like butterflies on a breeze,
soft moans, heavy exhalations, and quiet whimpering.
These expressions of felicity incite you
to intensify your feverish tongue-play.
Such sweet torment soon finds me writhing,
biting my hand to muffle cries of exultation.

Now, sailing up the coastline of my body,
you reach my still panting mouth for a leisurely kiss.
My breath slows to a contended rhythm
as you enfold me in protective arms.
Willowy limbs wrap around your sculpted frame
and we lie entangled in easy contentment.

Eventually, mutual craving rouses us to further play.
Your desirous hands trace over my curves,
admiringly, they travel ever downward,

drawn to the source of my sensuality.

At first, petting the silky down of dark gold
then boldly feeling between hidden folds.
Seeking the bud which is the key to my elation.
You bewitch me with the gentle way you handle
my most sensitive areas—always a tender touch.

My responsiveness prompts your fingers
to pursue a farther course, as my hand guides you.
You delve into the moisture that bedews your fingers.
My body receives you in a snug haven.

Your skillful fingers strum all my chords.
I am a harp to play with at your leisure.
Helpless, under the power of your hands
I elicit notes of sublime yearning,
which ignite the stars in the heavens
and cause tremors deep within the earth.

Transfixed by your stimulating talents,
I savor every creamy sensation.
With soft words you encourage me
to even higher states of bliss.
You quicken me with your urging voice,
exhilarating my emotions as I start to peak,
talking sweetly during the joyous convulsions
until the hot flood of euphoria begins to ebb away.
My never-ending thirst for shuddering ecstasy
is slaked momentarily but still not quenched.

3.

Now, my intent is to gratify you...relentlessly.
I brush my fingers along your primed virility,
smoothly sliding my hand up and down.
My light grasp strokes your naked flesh—

(Continued on page 34)

so supple in contrast to the firmness beneath.

Practiced fingers, skilled in technique
through familiarity with pleasing your body
perform acts of loving finesse—fondling, massaging,
rubbing in subtle circles over your most erogenous spot.
I keenly watch your spontaneous responses
to my indulgent gestures—an offering of devotion.
Attentive to the pulsing masculinity that I hold,
my carnal wisdom imparts that you are prepared
for a tantalizing encounter of deeper intimacy.

My gifted mouth replaces accomplished hands.
Tongue flicking at the apex of your promontory,
then swirling downward to the base,
spanning all that well-known territory.
My mouth admits you into its secluded cove,
at first only partly, while my generous tongue,
still giving liberally, brushes against your taut skin.
Long savoring licks, then skimming along the landscape,
finally short but strong lapping, enthralls your senses.
I press gingerly with my lips on that secret location
of which I have vast personal knowledge.

I stare, captivated, at your enamored face.
Your fair countenance is a divine vision—
parted lips tremble, long exhalations shudder,
eyes roll back beneath fluttering lids,
exclamations of joy chanted in exotic speech rush forth.

I allow you in deeper, sucking and stroking.
My mouth works dotingly at its task,
whetting your excitement, tending the lusty flame.
I can feel your manhood become doubly rigid,
the length and girth expanding further than I dreamed.
My instinctive reactions is to steadily swallow
all the throbbing hardness that fills my mouth.

I peer seductively up at you, holding you in my throat,
then increase the swiftness of my nodding motions,
dipping and raising from foundation to pinnacle.
You begin to flex involuntarily within me,
approaching the point of release.
As I catch your glazed eye, a provocative wink
signals the final motion in this symphony of sensations.

My tongue sweeps under your ridge—
spiraling, twisting, undulating, prodding.
Staccato cries, wild in nature, issue unrestrained
as tremors rock your whole body—
a nude panorama of chiseled musculature
that clenches just before the shockwave takes you.
Your vehement passion is finally unleashed
in an outpour of milky richness that I zealously drink,
but not before I taste the full flavor of a mouthful.

You rest as I curl up with you in an intimate embrace.
Your sculpted arms drape across my slim waist.
I cherish this time between phases of merrymaking,
relaxing with my paramour before a new venture.
However, the lull does not last long.

4.

A flirtatious kiss changes to a concentrated explosion
of renewed energy, becoming an erotic display.
Guiding me to your arms, in your genteel manner,
instinctively knowing how to handle my body,
Waiting respectfully for me to relinquish control,
though you yearn to cross the threshold of my entryway.

I am ready for you; I wish for us to join together.
You ease into me, pushing gently,
greeted by my receptive femininity.
I receive you into the cozy chamber of my sanctuary,

(Continued on page 36)

which stretches to accommodate
your enhanced manhood, in its entirety.

You begin delving into the source of my inviting heat,
such a commanding presence you wield
like a potent force driving into me.
Love-linked in utopian revelry, we merge in unity
like the blending of a harmonious medley.
We share mutual enjoyment as you possess my body.
I am emotionally fulfilled by your supportive love.
So I feel safe enough to liberate my soul
by abandoning limitations for a time.

I put you to the task, testing your physical exertions
with vigorous activity and heroic feats.
The action intensifies and quickens.
I am impressed with your epic performance.
I reach the height of heaven countless times
until paradise begins to feel familiar.
Yet, as always, I wish to return home
to where our bodies and spirits are bonding.

I arrive once more from Elysian transport
and note that you are reigning yourself in,
prolonging our play by delaying the moment of release.
I yearn to feel you ride the untamed outburst
of all your restraint to its conclusion.
Moaning my encouragement, I clench down,
tightening my grip until you are at the edge of rapture.
Hurried breath changes to unfettered shouts of jubilation,
as you lose composure in that revelatory moment.

Our sense of achievement lingers
as the shuddering from our exertions subsides.
Purring with satisfaction, I snuggle up to you.
You fulfill all promises of bliss as you hold me,
basking in the afterglow of a romantic caprice.

www.ingramcontent.com/pod-product-compliance
Lightning Source LLC
LaVergne TN
LVHW061226100826
845148LV00004B/876

* 9 7 8 0 9 8 2 3 6 3 1 9 5 *